SUPER
SANDCASTLE·
State Stories

THE GREAT LEI RACE

~ A Story About Hawaii ~

Written by Mary Elizabeth Salzmann

Illustrated by Bob Doucet

Consulting Editor, Diane Craig, M.A./Reading Specialist

ABDO
Publishing Company

Published by ABDO Publishing Company
8000 West 78th Street, Edina, Minnesota 55439.

Printed in the United States of America, North Mankato, Minnesota
112009
012010

 PRINTED ON RECYCLED PAPER

Editor: Katherine Hengel
Content Developer: Nancy Tuminelly
Cover and Interior Design: Anders Hanson, Mighty Media
Production: Colleen Dolphin, Mighty Media
Photo Credits: iStockphoto (Andrew Hill, Benjamin Lin,
Robin O'Connell, Martina Webster), One Mile Up,
SeaPics.com (D. R. Schrichte), Shutterstock.
Quarter-dollar coin image from the United States Mint.

Library of Congress Cataloging-in-Publication Data

Salzmann, Mary Elizabeth, 1968-
  The Great Lei Race : a story about Hawaii / Mary Elizabeth Salzmann ;
illustrated by Bob Doucet.
    p. cm.
  ISBN 978-1-60453-923-3
  1. Hawaii--Juvenile literature. I. Doucet, Bob, ill. II. Title.

DU623.25.S24 2010
996.9--dc22
                              2009033788

Super SandCastle™ books are created by a team of professional
educators, reading specialists, and content developers around
five essential components—phonemic awareness, phonics,
vocabulary, text comprehension, and fluency—to assist young
readers as they develop reading skills and strategies and
increase their general knowledge. All books are written,
reviewed, and leveled for guided reading, early reading
intervention, and Accelerated Reader® programs for use in
shared, guided, and independent reading and writing activities
to support a balanced approach to literacy instruction.

TABLE OF CONTENTS

luau
(pg. 19)

reef triggerfish
(pg. 17)

humpback whale
(pg. 4)

Hanalei

KAUAI

Kapaa

NIHAU

sea cliffs
(pg. 14)

OAHU

Wahiawa

Honolulu

Kalaupapa

MOLOKAI

nene
(pg. 7)

Pearl Harbor
(pg. 16)

LANAI

MAUI

Lahaina

POINT BELOW
FIRE ABOVE

Shipwreck Beach
(pg. 12)

Kihei

KAHOOLAWE

LEGEND

☆ CAPITAL   ● STORY START

○ CITY

- - - STORY PATH   ✖ STORY END

spinner dolphin
(pg. 13)

Hilo

Captain
Cook

HAWAII

Hawaiian monk seal
(pg. 5)

Humpback Whale

The humpback whale is Hawaii's state **marine mammal**. Many humpback whales live near Hawaii in the winter. In the summer, they move to cooler waters near Alaska.

THE GREAT LEI RACE

Hannah the humpback whale just got back to Hawaii after spending the summer in Alaska. She hasn't seen her very best friend Millie in months! "Hannah! Over here!" Hannah looks around. It's Millie the monk seal!

Hannah swims over to Millie as fast as she can. "Hi, Millie! I missed you this summer!"

"I'm so glad you're back, Hannah! The Great Lei Race starts tomorrow. Do you want to be a team?"

"I sure do, Millie! Let's meet at the starting line."

Hawaiian Monk Seal

Hawaii's state **mammal** is the Hawaiian monk seal. It is an **endangered species**. There are only about 1,200 Hawaiian monk seals left. All of them live in the Hawaiian Islands.

5

Hawaii, the Big Island

The state of Hawaii is made up of eight major islands and 124 very small islands. The largest island is also called Hawaii. People often call Hawaii the Big Island. Hilo is the largest city on the Big Island. It is located on the shore of Hilo Bay.

The next morning, the race teams gather in Hilo Bay. Mr. Naka the nene explains the rules. "Follow the clues to five secret locations. When you find each secret location, you will get a lei and the next clue."

Mr. Naka continues, "The race ends at Hanalei Beach on Kauai. The first team to arrive with all five leis wins! The first clue is on the board behind this sheet. The race begins as soon as I uncover the clue. Good luck!" He pulls off the sheet. The clue is POINT BELOW FIRE ABOVE.

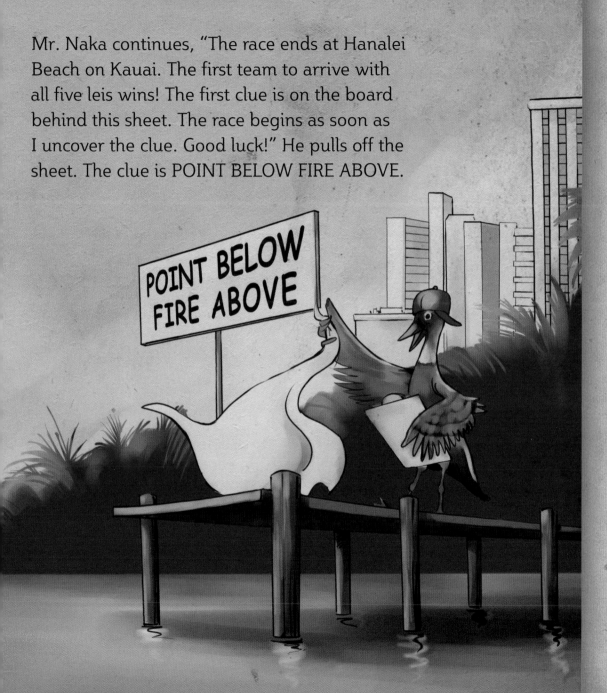

Nene

The nene is also called the Hawaiian goose. It is the state bird of Hawaii. The nene is an **endangered species**. Special groups protect nenes. There are only about 1,000 nenes in Hawaii.

"What do you think it means?" asks Millie.

Hannah answers, "Fire above could mean Kilauea in Hawaii Volcanoes National Park. There is usually smoke and lava up there. But what do we point to?"

"I know!" exclaims Millie. "My family camped on a beach below Kilauea. It's called Apua Point. So, it's a point below the fire of Kilauea above!"

Hawaii Volcanoes National Park

Hawaii Volcanoes National Park is on the Big Island. There are two **volcanoes** in the park, Mauna Loa and Kilauea. Kilauea is the most active volcano in the world. **Lava** erupts out of it every day.

"Great idea, Millie!" says Hannah. They quickly swim around the Big Island to Apua Point.

Millie says, "There's Kale the sea turtle. Look, he has a pile of yellow hibiscus leis."

"You are the second team," says Kale. "Here is your lei. The next clue is on the board." The clue is MAUI CAPITAL.

Yellow Hibiscus

The Hawaii state flower is the yellow hibiscus. This flower is often used to make leis. A lei is a large necklace made of flowers, leaves, nuts, or shells. Hawaiians give leis as special gifts to visitors.

Lahaina, Maui

The city of Lahaina is on the island of Maui. Maui is the second largest island in the state of Hawaii. Today, the capital of Hawaii is Honolulu. But from 1820 to 1845, Lahaina was the state capital.

Millie lets Hannah wear the first lei. Then she says, "The capital of Hawaii is Honolulu. But Honolulu is on Oahu, not Maui. What could the clue mean?"

Hannah says, "Honolulu wasn't always the capital. We learned in school that the capital used to be Lahaina."

"And Lahaina is on Maui!" exclaims Millie. "We'd better get going. Lahaina is a long way from here." Millie and Hannah head for Maui. It is almost dark by the time they get to Lahaina. A bat named Alani greets them at the harbor.

"Aloha, girls! You're team number four. Here's your lei. Check the board for your next clue." The clue is UNDERWATER LONDON.

The Aloha State

Hawaii's nickname is "The Aloha State." *Aloha* is a Hawaiian word that has many meanings. It is often used to say hello or good-bye. It can also mean love, caring, mercy, and kindness. All of the meanings together make up the Spirit of Aloha.

Shipwreck Beach, Lanai

Shipwreck Beach is on the shore of Lanai. The *London*, an American ship, was carrying gold and silver when it sank there in 1826. Another famous wreck was a World War II Liberty Ship. Visitors can still see this ship's rusted **hull** sticking out of the water!

"London!" Hannah yells. "Isn't that in England? I'm not swimming that far!"

"No, silly," says Millie. "It must be somewhere in Hawaii. What's underwater around here?"

Hannah replies, "Well, there's fish and shipwrecks and **reefs**."

Millie stops her. "That's it, Hannah! Shipwreck Beach! One of the ships that sank near there was called the *London*."

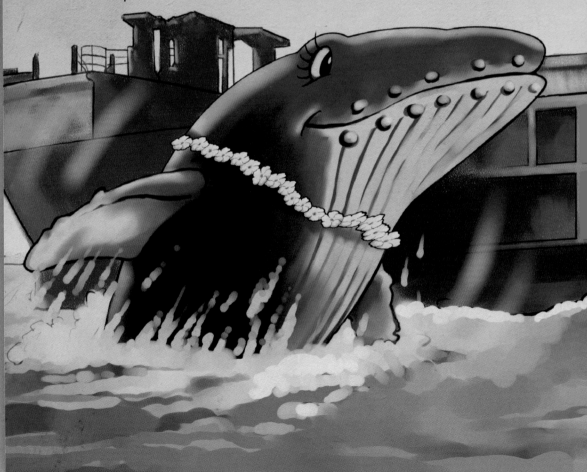

They decide to spend the night in Lahaina. The next morning, Hannah says, "Let's hurry! Maybe we'll pass the other teams." It doesn't take them long to get to Shipwreck Beach.

They see Lono the dolphin leaping and spinning. He says, "Aloha! You're in third place. Take a lei and read the board." The clue is TALLEST SHORE.

Spinner Dolphin

The spinner dolphin is very **acrobatic**. It can leap out of the water and spin around up to seven times! It can also turn somersaults in the air.

Sea Cliffs, Molokai

The north side of Molokai has many cliffs. Some of them are more than 3,000 feet (900 m) high. They are the highest sea cliffs in the world. Kalaupapa is a village at the bottom of the cliffs.

"We can't measure every shore in Hawaii," says Millie. "That would take forever!"

"We don't have to," says Hannah. "Do you remember learning about the Molokai cliffs? They are the highest sea cliffs in the world. A cliff by the sea is a very tall shore."

"Excellent, Hannah! Let's try Kalaupapa. It's on the only flat land near the cliffs. That's probably the secret location."

Millie and Hannah swim along the sea cliffs. Soon they get to Kalaupapa. Ollie the owl greets them from a kukui tree. "Hoo-ray for yo-o-ou! You're in second place. Here is your lei. There's the board with the final clue." The clue is OAHU TREASURE.

Kukui Tree

The kukui tree is the state tree of Hawaii. It has nuts and small white flowers. Both the nuts and flowers are often used in leis. Hawaiians used to burn kukui nuts for light. That's why the kukui is also called the candlenut tree.

15

Pearl Harbor, Oahu

Pearl Harbor is on the island of Oahu. Most of the harbor is a United States Navy base. During World War II, the Japanese army bombed Pearl Harbor. The Pearl Harbor Museum and USS *Arizona* Memorial teach visitors about the history of Pearl Harbor.

"Treasure!" Hannah exclaims. "Like gold and jewels? Do you think the location is a bank or a jewelry store?"

"Maybe," replies Millie. "But a pearl is a kind of jewel, right? What if we're supposed to go to Pearl Harbor?"

"Good idea, Millie!" says Hannah.

Millie says, "There's only one team in front of us. Let's see if we can catch them!" At Pearl Harbor, Emma the **gecko** meets them at the USS *Arizona* Memorial.

"Here's your fifth lei," she says. "Nia and Mia the triggerfish twins just left. You'd better hurry if you want to win!"

Reef Triggerfish

The **reef** triggerfish is Hawaii's state fish. It lives in and around coral reefs in shallow water. To escape danger, a triggerfish goes into a hole. It uses its top and bottom **spines** to hold itself in place.

17

Hanalei Beach, Kauai

Hanalei Beach is one of the most beautiful beaches in Hawaii. Behind the beach are mountains with tall waterfalls. It is a popular place for swimming, surfing, fishing, and boating.

Hannah and Millie swim as fast as they can to Kauai. As they near Hanalei Bay, they see Nia and Mia. "Just a little faster, Millie!" shouts Hannah. At the last minute, Hannah and Millie pass the triggerfish twins. They won the Great Lei Race! Mr. Naka gives them each a special lei with a gold medal. Hannah and Millie cheer for the other teams as they finish.

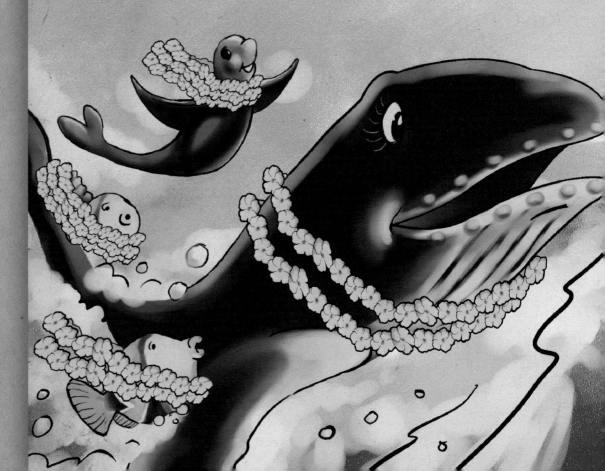

"I love the Great Lei Race," says Hannah. "Now it's time for the luau!"

"All right!" yells Millie. "I hope there's haupia. Let's go find out!"

THE END

Haupia (coconut pudding)

2 cups coconut milk

1 cup whole milk

6 tablespoons sugar

5 tablespoons cornstarch

¼ teaspoon vanilla (optional)

Heat 1 cup of coconut milk in a saucepan over low heat. Stir constantly while adding the sugar, cornstarch, and vanilla until thickened. Add remaining cup of coconut milk and whole milk. Stir until thickened. Pour into 8-inch square pan and chill until firm.

Luau

A luau is a Hawaiian feast. The main dish is usually a roasted pig. Hawaiian dishes such as **poi** and haupia are also often served. Hula dancing and drum and **ukulele** music are also common at luaus.

19

Hawaii at a Glance

Abbreviation: HI

Capital:
Honolulu, Oahu
(49th-largest U.S. city)

Largest city:
Honolulu, Oahu

Statehood: August 21, 1959 (50th state)

Area: 10,932 square miles (28,311 sq km) (43rd-largest state)

Nickname:
The Aloha State

Motto:
Ua mau ke ea o ka aina I ka pono. — The life of the land is perpetuated in righteousness.

State bird: nene

State flower: yellow hibiscus

State tree: kukui tree

State mammal:
Hawaiian monk seal

State marine mammal:
humpback whale

State fish: reef triggerfish

State song: "Hawai'i Pono'i" — Hawaii's Own

STATE SEAL

STATE FLAG

STATE QUARTER

The Hawaii quarter features Hawaiian King Kamehameha I. In the 1800s, King Kamehameha I united the islands under one government.

What Do You Know?

How well do you remember the story? Match the pictures to the questions below! Then check your answers at the bottom of the page!

 **a.** nene

 **b.** a kukui tree

 **c.** Kilauea Volcano

 **d.** Mia and Nia the triggerfish twins

 **e.** Millie the monk seal

 **f.** Lono the dolphin

1. Who is Hannah's best friend?

2. What kind of animal is Mr. Naka?

3. What is above Apua Point?

4. Who do Hannah and Millie meet at Shipwreck Beach in Lanai?

5. Where do Hannah and Millie find Ollie?

6. Who do Hannah and Millie beat to win the race?

What to Do in Hawaii

1 **VISIT A TROPICAL GARDEN**
Na 'Āina Kai Botanical Gardens, Kilauea, Kauai

5 **VIEW HAWAIIAN SEA LIFE UP CLOSE**
Maui Ocean Center, Ma'alaea Harbor, Maui

2 **TOUR THE ONLY ROYAL PALACE IN THE U.S.**
'Iolani Palace, Honolulu, Oahu

6 **EXPLORE A DORMANT VOLCANO**
Haleakala National Park, Maui

3 **HIKE TO A TROPICAL WATERFALL**
Halawa Valley and Moa'ula Falls, Molokai

7 **GO HORSEBACK RIDING**
Dahana Ranch, Waimea, Hawaii

4 **SWIM AND SNORKEL**
Hulopo'e Beach, Lanai

8 **STARGAZE ON MAUNA KEA**
Visitor Information Center, Mauna Kea, Hawaii

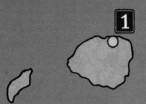

1

2

Honolulu

3

5

4

6

Hawaii

7

8

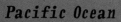

GLOSSARY

acrobatic – being very good at jumping, balancing, and other gymnastic acts.

endangered – when very few of a type of plant or animal are left in the world.

gecko – a small lizard.

hull – the body or frame of a ship or boat.

lava – hot, melted rock from inside a volcano.

mammal – a warm-blooded animal that has hair and whose females produce milk to feed their young.

marine – having to do with the sea.

poi – a Hawaiian food made of cooked taro root.

reef – a strip of coral, rock, or sand that is near the surface of the ocean.

species – a group of related living beings.

spine – a hard, sharp growth on a plant or animal.

ukulele – a type of small guitar that is popular in Hawaii.

volcano – a mountain that has lava and ash inside of it.

About SUPER SANDCASTLE™

Bigger Books for Emerging Readers
Grades K–4

Created for library, classroom, and at-home use, Super SandCastle™ books support and engage young readers as they develop and build literacy skills and will increase their general knowledge about the world around them. Super SandCastle™ books are part of SandCastle™, the leading PreK–3 imprint for emerging and beginning readers. Super SandCastle™ features a larger trim size for more reading fun.

Let Us Know

Super SandCastle™ would like to hear your stories about reading this book. What was your favorite page? Was there something hard that you needed help with? Share the ups and downs of learning to read. We want to hear from you! Send us an e-mail.

sandcastle@abdopublishing.com

Contact us for a complete list of SandCastle™, Super SandCastle™, and other nonfiction and fiction titles from ABDO Publishing Company.

www.abdopublishing.com • 8000 West 78th Street Edina, MN 55439 • 800-800-1312 • 952-831-1632 fax